S0-DXK-732

HOUGHTON MIFFLIN

Reading

A Legacy of Literacy

Spring Is Here

HOUGHTON MIFFLIN

BOSTON • MORRIS PLAINS, NJ

California • Colorado • Georgia • Illinois • New Jersey • Texas

Printed in the U.S.A.

ISBN: 0-618-07490-2

3456789-BS-06 05 04 03 02 01 00

Design, Art Management, and Page Production: Studio Goodwin Sturges

Contents

Get Set! Play!

by Ann Spivey
illustrated by Darcia Labrosse

 can get wet.
"Not yet," said .

Pig can get wet.
"Not yet," said Pig.

Fox can get wet.
"Not yet," said Fox.

 got a  .

Pig got  .

Fox got 3  .
Get set! Play!

Ben

by Ann Spivey
illustrated by Susan Calitri

"My pet!" said Ben.
"I can not get it."

"Get a net," said the vet.
Ben can not get it yet.

"Get a box," said Fox.
Ben can not get it yet.

"Get ten men," said Hen.
She got ten men.

Ten men got it.

Ben can play.

Pig Can Get Wet

by Ann Spivey
illustrated by Vincent Andriani

"My big wig can not get wet,"
said Pig. Pig sat.

"My big wig can not get wet."
Cat sat.

Cat can sit. Pig can sit.
A big  can not sit.

Cat got wet.
Pig got wet.

"A pig **can** get wet," she said.
"A pig can play."

Word List

Story 1: *Get Set! Play!*

Decodable Words

New

Consonant *w:* wet

Words with -*et:* get, set, wet, yet

Previously Taught
can, Fox, got, not, Pig

High-Frequency Words

New
play

Previously Taught
a, said

Word List

Story 2: *Ben*

Decodable Words

New

Consonant *y:* yet

Words with *-et, -en:* get, net, pet, vet, yet; Ben, Hen, men, ten

Previously Taught
box, can, Fox, got, it, not

High-Frequency Words

New
she

Previously Taught
a, I, my, said, play, the

Word List

Story 3: *Pig Can Get Wet*
Decodable Words
New
<u>Words with -*et*:</u> *get*, *wet*

Previously Taught
big, *can*, *Cat*, *got*, *not*, *Pig*, *sat*, *sit*, *wig*

High-Frequency Words
Previously Taught
a, *my*, *play*, *said*, *she*